# Mysteries Revealed

T0061953

Mari Bolte

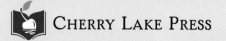

CHERRY LAKE PRESS

Published in the United States of America by Cherry Lake Publishing Group
Ann Arbor, Michigan
www.cherrylakepublishing.com

Reading Adviser: Beth Walker Gambro, MS, Ed., Reading Consultant, Yorkville, IL
Content Adviser: Robert S. Kowalczyk, MS, Physics, Systems Engineer (Retired) at the NASA Jet Propulsion Laboratory

Photo Credits: page 1: ©Xinhua News Agency/Contributor/Getty Images; page 5: ©NASA GSFC/CIL/Adriana Manrique Gutierrez/nasa.gov; page 6: ©dima_zel/Getty Images; page 9: ©mikroman6/Getty Images; page 10: ©NASA, ESA, CSA, STScI, Webb ERO Production Team/flickr.com; page 13: ©NASA, ESA, CSA, Leah Hustak (STScI)/Wikimedia; page 15: ©Roberto Colombari/Stocktrek Images/Getty Images; page 16: ©NASA, ESA, CSA, and J. Lee (NOIRLab). Image processing - A. Pagan (STScI)/flickr.com; page 19: ©GizemG/Shutterstock; page 20: ©NASA, ESA, CSA, and M. Zamani (ESA). Science: M. K. McClure (Leiden Observatory), F. Sun (Steward Observatory), Z. Smith (Open University), and the Ice Age ERS Team/flickr.com; page 22: ©NASA, ESA, K. Luhman and T. Esplin (Pennsylvania State University), et al., and ESO; Processing: Gladys Kober (NASA/Catholic University of America)/NASA.gov;  page 23: ©blueringmedia/Getty Images; page 25: ©Tom Masterson, ESO's DSS/nasa.gov; page 26: ©NASA, ESA, CSA, STScI, Klaus Pontoppidan (STScI), Image Processing: Alyssa Pagan (STScI)/flickr.com; page 28: ©NASA/Chris Gunn /nasa.gov; page 30: ©Pitris/Getty Images

Library of Congress Cataloging-in-Publication Data
Library of Congress Cataloging-in-Publication Data has been filed and is available at catalog.loc.gov.

ISBN 9781668938362 Lib.

Cherry Lake Publishing Group would like to acknowledge the work of the Partnership for 21st Century Learning, a Network of Battelle for Kids. Please visit Battelle for Kids online for more information.

Note from publisher: Websites change regularly, and their future contents are outside of our control. Supervise children when conducting any recommended online searches for extended learning opportunities.

Printed in the United States of America

**Mari Bolte** is an author and editor of children's books in every subject imaginable. She hopes the next generation sets their sights on the sky and beyond. Never stop the love of learning!

# CONTENTS

# CHAPTER 1

# Seeing into Space

The *James Webb Space Telescope* is on a mission. That mission began on December 25, 2021, when it was launched into outer space. *Webb* was equipped with four scientific instruments. They use near-**infrared** and mid-infrared to see what has never been seen before. Then *Webb* is able to send photos of those things back to Earth.

*Webb* is an **observatory** orbiting the Sun. In fact, it's the most powerful telescope in the sky. But it's more than that. It's a time machine that can see back close to the beginning of the universe. It's a camera. It's a **probe**. And it can look in almost any direction. It is currently 1 million miles (1.6 million kilometers) from Earth.

*Webb* is making new discoveries every day. It has shown scientists the early days of the universe. It has spotted

*Webb*'s mission will last for at least 5 years, with a goal of 10 years. But it has enough fuel to remain in orbit for more than 20!

never-before-seen galaxies. It has examined an enormous planet called a gas giant. This gas giant is 10 times more massive than Jupiter, the largest planet in our solar system. *Webb* snapped a picture of its first exoplanet in January 2023. These were only the first of many discoveries. Maybe one of those exoplanets will be explored by humans in the future. Space is full of mysteries—and *Webb* is working to reveal them.

# James Webb Facts

*Webb* can see some of the FIRST GALAXIES. Scientists can learn what the universe was like 13.8 billion years ago.

*Webb*'s cameras can take **deep-field** images. These images are taken by collecting light from the same region for long periods of time. This helps reveal FAINTER OBJECTS.

The Milky Way Galaxy has anywhere between 100 AND 400 BILLION stars. There are billions more stars and galaxies that we don't know about!

# CHAPTER 2

# The Eight-Legged Nebula

Some people are scared of tarantulas and webs. Others explore them! The Tarantula Nebula is more than 1,000 **light-years** across. And it's only around 160,000 light-years away. Luckily, it was only given its name because it looks like a giant tarantula—not because it is one.

Nebulae are clouds of space dust. This dust is not the same kind of dust on Earth. Space dust is formed in stars. It is blown off of older stars and during massive star explosions. Solar winds carry the dust into space. The dust is pulled together thanks to gravity. Eventually, the bits come together and form a mass. The mass becomes hot and dense. Eventually, a star is born. The Tarantula Nebula is where star birth is happening rapidly.

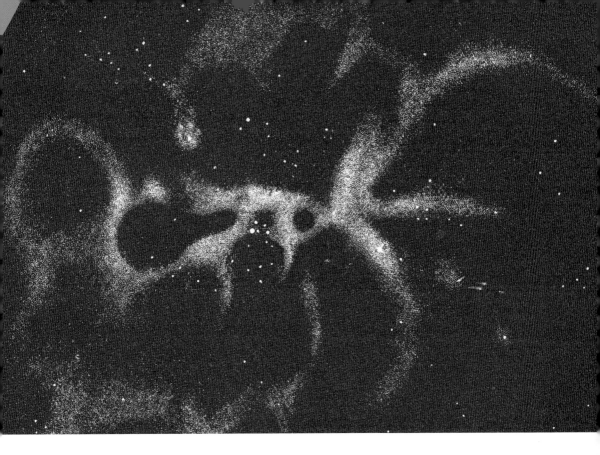

An engraving of the Tarantula Nebula clearly shows the cloud's "tarantula legs."

Details about the life cycle of stars are still very much a mystery. A period called Cosmic Noon happened 3 million years after the **Big Bang**. Most of the stars and black holes in our universe were created during this time. The activity in the Tarantula Nebula is similar to what occurred during Cosmic Noon. The stars born in our Milky Way don't have the same chemical makeup as stars in the Tarantula Nebula. It also does not make them as fast. Being able to look at the Tarantula Nebula gives scientists a better idea of how Cosmic Noon stars were made.

The Tarantula Nebula is also known as 30 DORADUS. It was first observed in the early 1750s by astronomer Nicolas Louis de Lacaille.

Lacaille couldn't see any stars with his telescope. The TARANTULA LEGS would not be seen until the 20th century.

There are more than 800,000 known stars in the Tarantula Nebula.

# Tarantula Nebula Facts

The Tarantula Nebula and the Milky Way are both part of the Local Group. Everything around us within about 5 million light-years is part of this Local Group. Astronomer Edwin Hubble named the Local Group in 1936. He was measuring distances between galaxies. There are around 30 galaxies in this area. The Tarantula Nebula is the largest stellar nursery in the Local Group.

Scientists have been studying the Tarantula Nebula for a long time. Technology, including telescopes like *Webb*, has helped scientists understand how stars are born and change over time.

In September 2022, *Webb* snapped a photo of the Tarantula Nebula with its Near-Infrared Camera (NIRCam) Instrument. NIRCam is *Webb*'s primary instrument. It can take pictures of faint things around bright objects. And nothing in the Local Group is brighter than the massive star cluster at the center of the nebula.

Hot, young stars put out radiation and stellar winds. The radiation and wind hollowed out the clouds at the center of the image. The light, bright blue coloring in the middle are those stars. The eight long "legs" of the tarantula are space dust and gas being blown around by the wind. The densest areas can resist the winds. These pillars are full of young protostars. The stars will eventually emerge and become part of the nebula.

LHS 475 b is in the constellation Octans. From Earth, it can only be seen from the Southern Hemisphere.

# NEW WORLDS

One of the great mysteries humans want to solve is finding out what else is out there. *Webb* discovered its first exoplanet in January 2023. Exoplanets are any planets outside our solar system. Many exoplanets orbit stars—much like how Earth orbits the Sun. Scientists have discovered thousands of exoplanets. With *Webb*'s help, they hope to find many more. There are around 200 billion trillion known stars out there. Scientists believe that there are just as many planets.

The exoplanet *Webb* discovered is nearly the same size as Earth. It is a rocky planet. The exoplanet orbits a star about 40 light-years away. There is one big difference, though. LHS 475 b is several hundred degrees hotter than Earth. However, its star is less than half the temperature of the Sun. Learning more about this exoplanet—and others—could answer the question, "Are we alone in the universe?"

# CHAPTER 3

# Gas, Dust, and Galaxies

Galaxies are more than just random dots in the sky. Galaxies are classified into four types. They are **elliptical**, grand design spiral, barred spiral, and irregular. One of *Webb*'s missions is to survey 19 spiral galaxies. Scientists are not sure what the galaxies will reveal. However, they hope that whatever they find helps us understand our universe.

In February 2023, *Webb*'s Mid-Infrared Instrument (MIRI) targeted NGC 1433. It's a barred spiral galaxy around 46 million light-years away. The image looked like a bright core surrounded by a double oval-shaped ring of light. The rings are the galaxy's spiral arms. Young stars release a lot of light energy. This energy is absorbed by dust and gas. The energy can be seen as infrared waves that can be picked up by MIRI.

NGC 3314 is a "galaxy pair" of two overlapping spiral galaxies, shown in this photo with artistic alterations.

MIRI is one of *Webb*'s four on-board instruments. It is the only one that can see in mid-infrared light. MIRI can detect **wavelengths** longer than what the human eye can see. It can see cool, distant galaxies that are moving away from us due to the expanding universe. This is called redshift. MIRI can also see through space dust to show scientists new stars and comets. And it can gaze through space dust, which can hide stars from other telescopes.

# NGC 1433 Facts

The image *Webb* took is bright. Scientists believe this means NGC 1433 RECENTLY MERGED with another galaxy.

The navy blue, pink, red, and white dots on the GALAXY'S ARMS are also space dust.

# CHAPTER 4

# Bursting Through the Sky

Space is dark. It's cloudy. But there are also hints of brightness. As galaxies form and change, space dust is created. That dust blows throughout the galaxy. It merges with an odorless, colorless gas called **molecular** hydrogen. They turn into molecular clouds and can become stellar nurseries. Inside these nurseries are patches of cloud matter called Herbig-Haro objects. These objects are created by newborn stars pushing dust and gas into space.

Chameleon 1 is a molecular cloud. It is so thick that it hides whatever was inside. The cloud is full of ice. But it's not just the kind of ice you probably think of. Frozen carbon dioxide, ammonia, methane, and methanol are also there. They freeze to bits of dust inside the cloud, which makes it even harder to see. These molecules all have different

Young stars inside stellar nurseries create solar winds, which can reach speeds of more than 1 million miles (1.6 million km) per hour. Parts of this image were taken by NASA, with artistic alterations.

freezing points. The coldest parts of Chameleon 1 can reach temperatures as low as −440 degrees Fahrenheit (−262 degrees Celsius).

Eventually, these molecules and the interstellar hydrogen will join to create the hot core of a new star. They might even become part of an exoplanet. These elements contain the building blocks needed for a habitable world. These blocks are carbon, oxygen, hydrogen, nitrogen, and sulfur, also known as COHNS.

# Chameleon 1 Facts

The Chameleon 1 dark molecular cloud is 630 TO 650 LIGHT-YEARS away.

CHAMELEON 1 is also called Cha 1 for short. There are also Chameleons 2 and 3.

Together, the clouds are 65 LIGHT-YEARS across.

*Hubble* photographed Chameleon 1 in 2022. This picture was compiled from 23 different observations.

Every element in a molecular cloud absorbs different wavelengths of light. By measuring the wavelengths, scientists can figure out exactly what elements make up the cloud. *Webb* can do that. Its infrared cameras can see what human eyes can't.

The cold, cloudy center is blue. It glows thanks to the young protostar in the upper left-hand corner of the image on the previous spread. The light from other background stars can be seen as orange dots. It is absorbed by the cloud's ice, showing scientists the colder, denser parts.

# James Webb Space Telescope

**Primary Mirror:** Made up of 18 smaller mirrors that work together to pick up light from long distances and focus on distant objects

**Secondary Mirror:** Reflects gathered light from the main mirror to the science instruments

**Science Instruments:** Four instruments that take photos called spectrograph—they also take precise measurements of infrared and near-infrared light from objects in space

**Sunshield:** Keeps the telescope cool on the side that faces the Sun

**Antenna:** Sends data back to Earth twice a day

# CHAPTER 5

# One Year in the Sky

*Webb*'s first color images were released in July 2022. The mountains and peaks of the Cosmic Cliffs dazzled astronomy fans around the world. That was just the start. Every image *Webb* took was a new discovery. Mysteries were one step closer to being solved. But other new mysteries came to light! Science is all about finding answers. *Webb's* goal is to search for the first galaxies, find out about how stars, planets, and galaxies form, and if there's a chance that other life is out there.

On July 21, 2023, NASA released *Webb*'s picture of Rho Ophiuchi. It's an active star-forming nursery 390 light-years away. The nursery is small. *Webb*'s photo, on the following spread, brings it to life. Jets from young stars burst across the center, pushing away the interstellar gas in their path.

The Rho Ophiuchi cloud complex has enough material to form 3,000 stars the size of our Sun. This image was taken in 2016 by the ESO Online Digitized Sky Survey, with artistic alterations.

Molecular hydrogen is shown as red jets in the upper right-hand corner. This is a necessary ingredient in new star birth.

The black shadows around the red jets are accretion disks. These are flattened disks of gas and dust that rotate around a body in space. The body is most often a star. But sometimes, they can lead to the creation of a planet.

# Rho Ophiuchi Facts

It is part of the constellation OPHIUCHUS (off-ee-YOO-kus). The name means "serpent bearer."

RHO OPHIUCHI is the closest star-forming nebula to Earth.

Ophiuchus is the 11TH LARGEST constellation in our sky. The Greek astronomer Ptolemy recorded it in the 2nd century.

*Webb*'s mirror is covered in a thin layer of gold. The gold helps in the reflection of infrared light.

*Webb*'s large mirror is made up of smaller, hexagon-shaped mirrors. Each mirror has six sides. This causes the **diffraction** spikes around bright stars. Each mirror side creates a spike. There are also two smaller spikes. These are from a support piece on the telescope itself. Look closely at the stars in the image of Rho Ophiuchi on the previous spread. Can you see all the spikes?

The image shows around 50 stars as massive as our own Sun scattered through Rho Ophiuchi's clouds. Most are near the center. These are young stars. But the cloud isn't done yet. There's enough gas and dust in the cloud to create 3,000 Suns! The biggest star in the image is called S1. Its stellar winds are carving a cave in the cloud. Other carbon-containing gases surround the star.

There is a lot that science doesn't yet know about star birth. It's a short-lived period in a star's life. It's easy to miss. Thanks to *Webb*, though, scientists can capture that moment in time. Then they can go back later to compare how things have changed. *Webb* has collected a lot of new information. But there is still a lot out there that's unknown! Every photo brings us one step closer to solving another space mystery.

# THE NEXT GENERATION

*Webb*'s cameras have been tested. They have shown off what they can do. And they will continue to study the sky. It was once known as the *Next Generation Space Telescope*. Although the name was changed to the *James Webb Space Telescope* in 2002, it's still accurate.

*Webb* has been working with other organizations and space telescopes. The *Hubble Space Telescope* was launched in 1990. It should operate until at least 2040. The *Nancy Grace Roman Space Telescope* is scheduled to launch by 2027. Both *Webb* and *Hubble* look at tight, concentrated parts of the sky. *Roman* will take huge panoramic shots. They will be 200 times larger than *Hubble*'s. The images will be used to make a 3D model of the universe.

Combining *Webb*, *Roman*, and *Hubble* will help scientists solve some of the universe's biggest mysteries. Maybe someday, what we learn will lead to stepping foot on a new world.

# Activity

## Connect to STEAM: Science

*Webb* will send data back to Earth for years to come. There are many things we can learn from that information. But what would you want to learn? Think of questions you want to answer or theories you want to test. How could *Webb* help answer them?

Pretend you are a scientist working for NASA. Start with the ideas below. Then expand on them! Finally, present your ideas to others. Hear their ideas and add suggestions. Did you learn anything new? Did it change any of your ideas?

- How big is the universe?
- How do galaxies start?
- Are there any exoplanets similar to Earth, or is Earth totally unique?
- How fast is the universe expanding?
- What did the first stars look like?

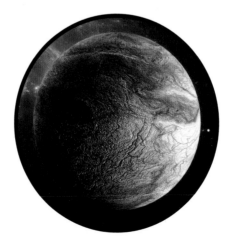

# Find Out More

## Books

Bolte, Mari. *Space Discoveries*. Ann Arbor, MI: Cherry Lake Publishing, 2022.

Collins, Ailynn. *Super Surprising Trivia about Space and the Universe*. North Mankato, MN: Capstone Press, 2024.

Lombardo, Jennifer. *Do Other Earths Exist?* Buffalo, NY: Enslow Publishing, 2023.

Reeves, Diane Lindsey. *James Webb Space Telescope: A Peek into the First Galaxies*. Minneapolis: Lerner Publications, 2024.

## Online Resources to Search with an Adult

European Space Agency: Exoplanets

NASA Space Place: Telescope

Nine Planets: Exoplanets Planets Facts for Kids

What Is the *James Webb Telescope*?

# Glossary

**Big Bang** (BIG BAYNG) an explosion that scientists believe started the formation of the universe

**deep-field** (DEEP FEELD) a type of image taken by collecting light from the same region for long periods of time

**diffraction** (di-FRAK-shuhn) when a beam of light is bent or spread out

**elliptical** (ih-LIP-tik-uhl) oval-shaped

**exoplanet** (EKS-oh-plan-uht) a planet that orbits a star outside the solar system

**infrared** (in-fruh-RED) invisible light from beyond the red end of the visible light spectrum

**light-years** (LYTE-YEERZ) units of distance equal to how far light travels in 1 year—6 million miles (9.6 trillion km)

**molecular** (muh-LEK-yoo-luhr) made of extremely small particles

**observatory** (ob-ZUR-vuh-tor-ee) a place used for watching outer space

**probe** (PROHB) an unpiloted spacecraft that travels through space to collect information

**protostars** (PROH-toh-stahrs) very young stars that are still forming

**stellar** (STEH-luhr) relating to stars

**wavelengths** (WAYV-lengths) measurements between one wave to another as energy flows through space in a wavelength pattern

# Index